the ROYAL CANADIAN mounted POLICE

ILLUSTRATED BY MARC TÉTRO

Scholastic Canada Ltd.

Scholastic Canada Ltd.
123 Newkirk Road, Richmond Hill, Ontario, Canada L4C 3G5

Scholastic Inc.
555 Broadway, New York, NY 10012, USA

Ashton Scholastic Limited
Private Bag 94407, Greenmount, Auckland, New Zealand

Ashton Scholastic Pty Limited
PO Box 579, Gosford, NSW 2250, Australia

Scholastic Publications Ltd.
Villiers House, Clarendon Avenue, Leamington Spa
Warwickshire CV32 5PR, UK

*Thanks to Malcolm J. H. Wake, director of the Museum of The Royal Canadian Mounted Police,
for his help during my visit to Regina;
to Victoria Wonnacott, my assistant, for her meticulous research;
and finally, to Dale Horeczy, my partner,
who assisted in every aspect of the publication of this book.*

Marc Tétro and Martin Loranger co-authored the text of the French edition of this book
which was used in part in preparing this English edition.

Graphic design: Christopher Cant

5 4 3 2 1   Printed in Canada   5 6 7 8/9

Canadian Cataloguing in Publication Data

Tétro, Marc, 1960–
The Royal Canadian Mounted Police

Issued also in French under title: La Gendarmerie
royale du Canada.

ISBN 0-590-24544-9

1. Royal Canadian Mounted Police – History –
Juvenile literature. I. Title.

FC3216.T4713 1995   j363.2'0971 C95-930669-2
FI060.9.T4713 1995

*To all the grandparents
who've ever wanted to tell the story
of the Royal Canadian Mounted Police
to their grandchildren.*

the ROYAL CANADIAN mounted Police

More than
a hundred years ago,
on the vast
Canadian prairie,
lived the country's
first people.

They lived in teepees,
houses they could
quickly pack up
when they wanted to follow
the herds of bison.

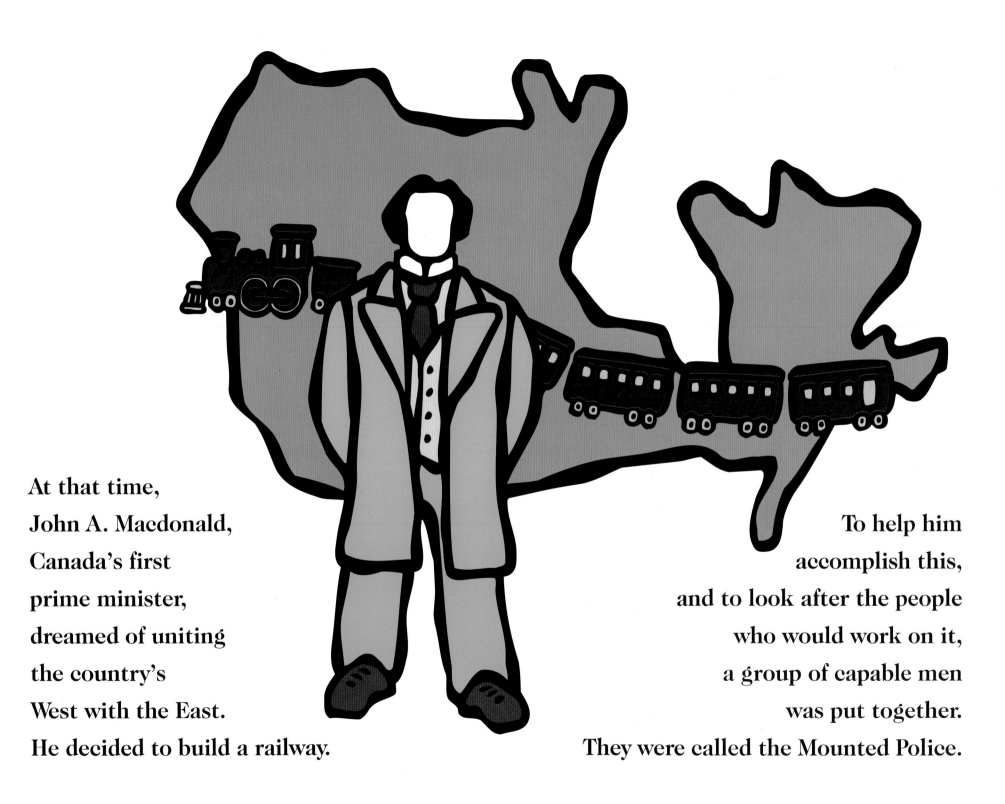

At that time,
John A. Macdonald,
Canada's first
prime minister,
dreamed of uniting
the country's
West with the East.
He decided to build a railway.

To help him
accomplish this,
and to look after the people
who would work on it,
a group of capable men
was put together.
They were called the Mounted Police.

Among the recruits,
there were
teachers and
farmers,
students and
lumberjacks.

The proud new Mounties were eager for adventure as they set out from Manitoba

for their long journey West. The land was beautiful, and it seemed to go on forever.
But it was also cruel. The sun burned down, the sky was filled with black-flies . . .

. . . and the animals were exhausted.

Finally, after two long months, the cavalcade reached the land of the Blackfoot.

The Mounties immediately
went to work building
their first outpost
in the West:
Fort Macleod.

With time, some of the Blackfoot elders
learned to trust these men in red tunics,
and an agreement was reached.
The train would now be allowed
to cross their land.

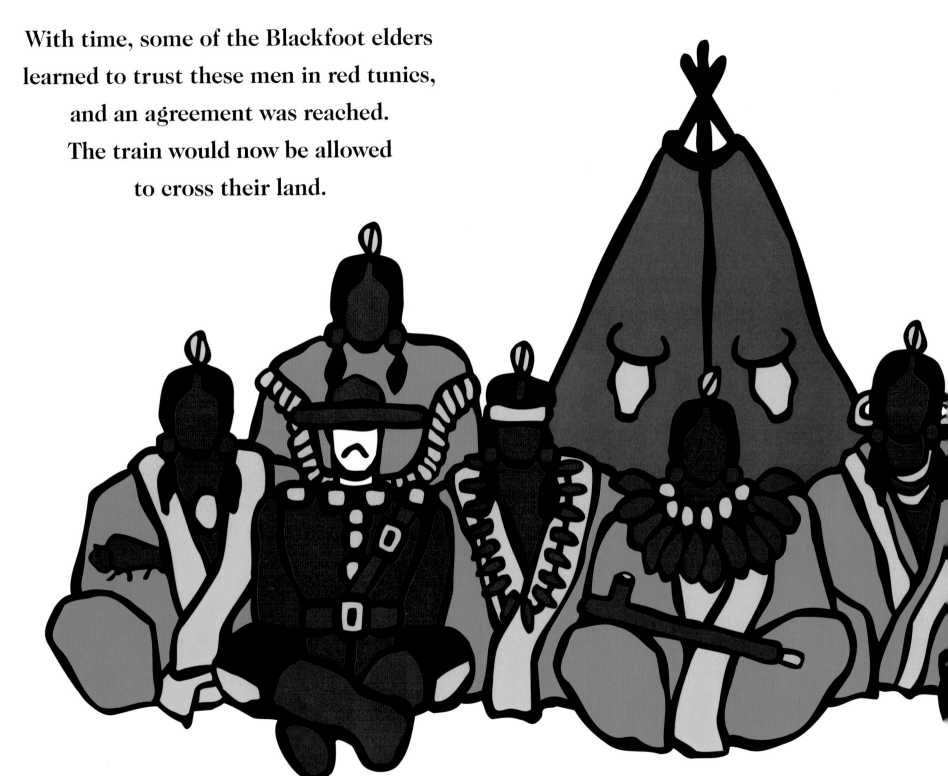

Later, Louis Riel, the leader of the Métis,
a people of French and Indian blood,
fought the division of his ancestors' land.
The Métis wanted their own country, but their dream was not to come true.

The workers began building the railway.

Soon, the first whistle of the Canadian Pacific train blew in the West. The train brought people

from eastern Canada, as well as Ukrainians, Poles and Germans from Europe.

There were houses to build,
fields to plough and a new way of life to learn.
The Mounties were there to help
the new families settle in.

15

The Mounties'
musical ride
entertained the
people in the
new communities.

Gold in the Klondike!
Thousands of men
rushed to the Yukon
hoping to strike it rich.

Dawson City went mad.
Men used
bad language,
played cards
and spent the night
dancing with the ladies.

But, of course,
the law
had to be
respected.

The Mounties
reached the Far North.
There, they met the Inuit.
These people
snuggled up in igloos,
houses that were
made of blocks of ice.
It was the Inuit who helped
the Mounties explore
the Canadian Arctic.

21

King Edward VII
recognised
the important work
the Canadian Mounties
were doing,
and he gave them
a royal title.

They become known
as the Royal North-West
Mounted Police.
Later, their name
was changed to
the Royal Canadian
Mounted Police.

23

Today, the Mounties
don't travel the country on horseback
as they did in the time of
John A. Macdonald.
But their work is just as important:
they're dedicated to
protecting Canadians by watching
over the country's borders,
from the Atlantic Provinces
to the Yukon.